I LOVE YOU, MAN . . . BUT NOT LIKE *THAT*

I LOVE YOU, MAN... BUT NOT LIKE THAT

If You Can't Insult Your Best Buddy... You're Probably Not a Guy

Greg Suess and D. M. Chapman

Andrews McMeel Publishing, LLC
Kansas City

I Love You, Man . . . but Not Like That

For information, write Andrews McMeel Publishing,
LLC, an Andrews McMeel Universal company,
4520 Main Street, Kansas City, Missouri 64111.

07 08 09 WKT 6 5 4 3 2

ISBN-13: 978-0-7407-6078-5
ISBN-10: 0-7407-6078-5

Library of Congress Control Number: 2006923258

www.andrewsmcmeel.com

To the love of my life, Michelle.
I love you like that.

–G

To Hop, Fro, and Hagerty . . .
the funniest guys I know.

–Cheers, D

CONTENTS

They say the greatest gift you can give another person is the gift of yourself. But really, I think a little book full of prewritten sentimental thoughts is a pretty good gift, too.

Because putting my deepest thoughts about friendship into words would be incredibly difficult. And yet, picking up this little book, conveniently located near the cash register and filled with all the kinds of things I might say anyway, is easy as pie.

Mmmm . . . pie.

It would be nearly impossible to put a price on our friendship. But as a ballpark figure, this book cost me about nine bucks.

CHAPTER •ONE•

Thoughts on Friendship

The greatest ship
the world has
ever known
is friendship.

The greatest chip
is the Dorito.

I bet if you were walking along the beach one day, and a magic genie suddenly appeared and offered you the greatest ship in the world, and you chose "friendship"...

That genie would kick your ass.

There is only
one plane on which
friendship can thrive,
and that is an
equal plane.

Or a really cool
private jet.

Because, let's face it,
if you've got your own
private plane you can
be a complete tool
and still have plenty
of friends.

Friendship doubles our joy, and friendship halves our sorrow.

Friendship divides the hardships in life and multiplies the blessings.

But the real question is . . . if friendship leaves Station A at 4:26, moving at a speed of 55 miles per hour, and arrives at Point B at 5:14, how many miles has friendship traveled?

A friend is a gift
you give yourself.

I tried regifting,
but nobody
wanted you.

True friendship is as sturdy as the mighty oak and has the power to move mountains.

So why is it that when I say "U-Haul" and "sofa bed," you're suddenly "busy" or "sick"?

A great friendship can be a source of inspiration and wonder.

For example, I recently wondered what the hell would inspire you to consistently make such an ass of yourself.

True friends outlast trends.

But seriously, dude, lose the sideburns.

CHAPTER •TWO•

Inspirational Thoughts

An interesting question people sometimes like to ask is, "If you could sit down and have a beer with just one man, living or dead, who would it be?"

I'd pick the living one.

True success in life is measured not by the material possessions we are able to acquire, but by the number of our friends...

Who envy
those material
possessions.

When the light of friendship brightens a man's day, he will, in turn, take that brightness and share it, and the light of friendship can spread to everyone he comes in contact with, and everyone they come in contact with, and so on, and so on. . . .

The light of friendship is sort of like herpes that way.

The greatest gift you ever give is the gift of yourself.

FYI . . . other people give actual gifts, cheapskate.

One good philosophy to live by is to try to live each day as if it were your last.

Quit your job, then run around weeping and shrieking, "Oh my God, I'm gonna die! I'm gonna die!"

If, on your deathbed, you can look back on your life and count five real friends, then you truly are a lucky man.

Except, you know,
for the whole
"deathbed" thing.

There are many ways to measure success, not the least of which is the way a child would describe you to a friend.

In your case, it would probably be something like "that funny-looking man who lives with his mommy."

CHAPTER •THREE•

Words of Wisdom

George Washington famously once stated that it is better to be alone than to be in bad company.

But hey, what the hell did he know? The guy had wooden teeth and stood up in boats.

My friend, if you ever find yourself in a time of trouble or despair, I'd like to share the inspirational, comforting words of my father, in response to my childhood tears . . .

"You wanna cry?
Huh? You wanna cry,
I'll give you something
to cry about!"

A wise man once said the companionship of a true friend is more valuable than gold.

But really, wouldn't that depend on *how much* gold?

One of the most important qualities of a true friend is that he is always willing to lend you his ear.

No, wait. Car. Always willing to lend you his car.

Leading researchers now say that one out of every two men will experience erectile dysfunction at some point during his lifetime.

Man, sucks to
be you, huh?

Recent findings have shown that consistently spending time with a good friend can produce feelings of euphoria, elation, and well-being.

Particularly when that friend has recently returned from Jamaica with a little something "extra" in his luggage.

"If you do the best you can, you will find, nine times out of ten, that you have done as well as or better than anyone else."

—WILLIAM FEATHER

But that tenth time,
you'll screw it up
so bad nobody will
ever remember
the other nine.

The power of thought is such that whatever a man is able to think, that man can become.

Which must
make you
the Invisible Man.

CHAPTER •FOUR•

Thank You . . .

For always making me look good.

By comparison.

Because laughter
is the best medicine . . .

And I can always count on you to do something really stupid so I can laugh at you.

For always being there for me. When I'm feeling blue, you're always around. When I have something to celebrate, you're right there beside me. When I need a helping hand, there you are.

But I've got to tell you, it's really starting to creep me out in the men's room.

Because every achievement is sweeter when shared with you, my friend.

I think it's the look of sick, churning envy on your face that does it.

For your undying willingness to "take one for the team"...

And hook up with
the hot chick's fat,
ugly friend.

Because every one of my wins would mean absolutely nothing if it weren't for you . . .

Being there to lose.

Because you should always take time to appreciate the simple things in life.

And there's nobody simpler than you.

CHAPTER

•FIVE•

You're Special!

(Which is why you got to ride to school on the short bus.)

You always keep your chin up and a grin on your face . . . even when you've been dumped again, or lost your job, or are feeling the effects of having had one too many the night before.

Which is probably why people often ask me, "What the hell does that alcoholic, unemployed loser have to be so darn giddy about?"

I recently heard someone compare you to one of the most brilliant minds of the last century.

I think their
actual words were
"Well, he's no Einstein."

One thing I love about you is the way you always rise to a challenge.

For example, when companies refer to something as "idiot-proof," you always manage to prove them wrong.

I have to say, you may not be the most successful friend I've got . . .

Or the best looking.

Or the smartest.

I'm just saying.

When I first met you, it seemed like you could get pretty down on yourself, and I was worried that you had some sort of self-esteem issues or an inferiority complex.

But I soon realized your low opinion of yourself was actually an accurate assessment.

I overheard some really hot girls talking about you the other day at your gym. They said you had the physique of a Greek god.

The one that's
half goat.

If your neighbors were ever asked to describe you, I bet they'd have some pretty nice things to say.

Probably something like, "He was always real quiet . . . polite . . . kind of kept to himself."

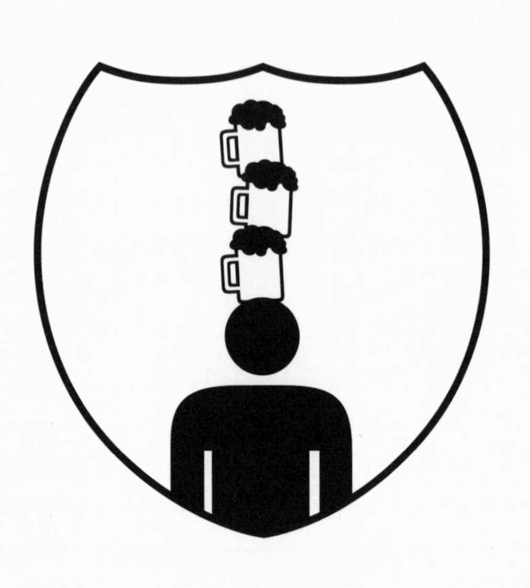

CHAPTER

•SIX•

You're Unique!

(Just like every other man, woman, and child around the world.)

There are very few people in this world like you.

No, wait. There are very few people in this world who like you.

You are one of the few people who truly follow that age-old advice to "just be yourself."

You might want to rethink that, compadre.

All too often we look right through those we spend time with every day, never really seeing them.

Recently, I looked at you, really looked at you, and thought . . .

It's truly shocking that any woman would ever have sex with someone with so much nose hair.

If, as they say, the best mirror is an old friend . . .

Then I have really let myself go.

A man must not deny his manifest abilities, for that is to evade his obligations.

Which I guess means you're obligated to shotgun beers and burp the Gettysburg Address.

In all of Creation,
throughout the history
of Mankind, there has
never been, and there
never will be, another
man exactly like you,
my friend.

But if you can convince people you have an evil twin, oh man, the things you can get away with.

CHAPTER

•SEVEN•

You're Great!

(No matter what your girlfriend, friends, boss, coworkers, parents, or anyone else says about you.)

Sometimes I find myself thinking about you and what a really great friend you are, and it makes me want to send you flowers or a big bunch of balloons or maybe a really nice muffin basket.

But then I realize that would be gay.

You have all the qualities I look for in a friend.

I enjoy

feeling superior.

My friendship with you reminds me of some of the greatest friendships throughout history.

B.J. and the Bear,
Clint and Clyde,
Reagan and Bonzo . . .

Our friendship has passed the test of time with flying colors.

But could it ever pass a Breathalyzer?

No matter what you might do to drive him away, a true friend keeps coming back.

Kind of like those suspicious sores you've been meaning to see the doctor about.

"If you can keep your head while all about you are losing theirs . . . then you'll be a Man, my son."

—RUDYARD KIPLING

And if you can keep your virginity while all about you are losing theirs . . .

Well, you tell me. What's that like?

CHAPTER
•EIGHT•

You've Touched Me

(No, seriously. We were both pretty drunk, but I have a definite recollection of you touching me.)

Whenever someone asks me why you and I are such good buddies, I usually just chuckle and tell them . . .

“I barely know that guy.”

After meeting you, my great-uncle Chuck said you're just the kind of man he'd like to have with him in a foxhole.

He was never in the war or anything, he just enjoys being in small, enclosed spaces with other men.

I was having a bad day recently, feeling overwhelmed with work and responsibilities. And then I got an e-mail from you, my friend, some joke or humorous cartoon, and I thought to myself . . .

"Why the hell does this moron keep forwarding me annoying crap when I'm overwhelmed with work and responsibilities?"

You're so cool to hang out with, I sometimes think if you were a girl I'd probably bang you.

But only if I was really bombed, because I bet you'd be a butt-ugly girl.

As you go through your day, always remember that you leave a little bit of yourself behind in each encounter with another person.

DNA, fingerprints,

fibers . . .

Our friendship is so strong that if you and I were stranded on a lifeboat and there was only enough food and water for one of us to survive . . .

I bet I'd feel pretty bad as I pushed you overboard.

CHAPTER

•NINE•

Memories

(Isn't it funny how it's always the memorable things that really stick with us?)

I often think about how much we've gone through together over the years . . .

And the fact that most of it was your fault.

I'll always cherish the memories of the unforgettable times we've spent together.

Like the time we went to that one place for that thingamajig with that guy, what's-his-name, and hung out with what's-her-face and the other chick.

Good times.

You've always been my favorite "partner in crime."

Except for that time you locked the keys in the getaway car, because, man, that was stupid.

If you got married, and I was your best man, I think I would tell the inspirational true story about the time I was riding my horse through the Colorado Rocky Mountains and I came upon a grove of Aspen trees that had all been bent and twisted by strong winds and bad weather.

All except one tree, in the middle, which stood straight and tall.

Intrigued, I rode closer so I could see what it was about this tree—what made it strong enough to withstand what its tree brethren could not?

And that was when I realized it wasn't one tree, but two trees, growing close together, their branches intertwined!

And I thought to myself that you and I were like those two trees, able to weather more together than either of us could dream of alone.

And by "horse," I mean futon. And by "Colorado Rocky Mountains," I mean my living room. And by "grove of Aspen trees," I mean a Web site called www.bestmanspeech.com.

Take heart, my friend, in knowing that whenever you turn to me in times of sadness, if you've lost your job, or your girl-friend, or your car, my first impulse is always to offer you reassurance and comfort.

Of course, I quickly squash that impulse and mock you mercilessly.

But still, don't you feel better knowing about that first impulse?

After all this time, I still feel as though we've barely even begun to explore the true depths of our friendship.

But then again, maybe you're just really shallow.

CHAPTER
•TEN•

Sports, Etc.

(We'll keep this one short, Champ, since I know sports aren't really your "thing.")

It's not whether you win or lose that matters, it's how you play the game.

In your case, pretty badly.

The other day, out on the course, as I watched you sink that difficult putt, I couldn't help but think to myself . . .

"Damn, his ass looks fat in those pants."

I'd like to invite you into my circle of trust and honesty. And now that you're here, I can honestly tell you . . .

You ought to get your fat, lazy ass into the gym, stripes don't "go" with plaid, and you desperately need a breath mint.

You can win only
if you're not afraid
to lose.

And you've clearly conquered that fear.

I have to tell you,
in many ways . . .
I consider you just
like my brother.

He throws like
a girl, too.

Even when you try your very best, there are still times when you come in second or third or even last.

And I just laugh
my ass off.

You know, I still remember sitting on my grandfather's knee, absorbing these classic words of male wisdom that I'll share with you now: "If you've played the game to the best of your abilities, there is no shame in losing . . ."

"Unless it's

to a girl."

We share so much in common—love of sports, beer, women—but I think you'll agree, deep down, our friendship is based on something more.

Proximity and convenience.

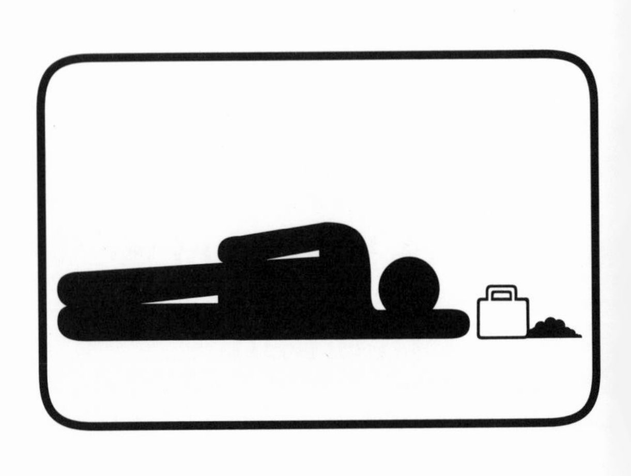

CHAPTER

•ELEVEN•

Last Call

I thought I would end with "Chapter Eleven" in order to remind you that our friendship account will always be rich with fond memories . . .

Even when you're morally, spiritually, and financially bankrupt.

And now, with all of the joking and mockery aside, I can quote that immortal source of wisdom, the almighty beer commercial, and say those four little words I generally only mumble incoherently right before vomiting on your shoes . . .

"I love you, man."

(But not like *that*.)